The Reality of Truth

The Reality of Truth

Poetic Healing for Victims of Abuse

Michael Rother and Kathy Schuetrum

iUniverse, Inc.
New York Lincoln Shanghai

The Reality of Truth
Poetic Healing for Victims of Abuse

iUniverse books may be ordered through booksellers or by contacting:

iUniverse
2021 Pine Lake Road, Suite 100
Lincoln, NE 68512
www.iuniverse.com
1-800-Authors (1-800-288-4677)

Because of the dynamic nature of the Internet, any Web addresses or links contained in this book may have changed since publication and may no longer be valid.

The views expressed in this work are solely those of the author and do not necessarily reflect the views of the publisher, and the publisher hereby disclaims any responsibility for them.

ISBN: 978-0-595-47577-3 (pbk)
ISBN: 978-0-595-91842-3 (ebk)

Printed in the United States of America

Special thanks to Jacci for typing everything. You are a very special person in our hearts and souls, with great thanks and appreciation.

Contents

PART II   HOPE

PART III   LOVE

I

Pain

"Therefore, encourage one another and build one another up just as you are doing."

I Thessalonians 5:11

Expect the Unexpected

When little girls have been raped and abused
Their crimes and their sins must be excused
Without the love of some one who cares
They get caught in all of life's snares

Some spend their lives being raped and abused
Respect and Dignity they are refused
Some find Love and live lives that are good
They all just want to be understood

I write for those who have been raped and abused
Beaten and tortured and totally used
My words are filled with love and respect
'Cause that is something they never expect

Loneliness

You feel you are the only one
Who knows how sad life can be
Take a look around this world
There are so many smiles to see

End of the World

People dying children crying,
End of the world is near
The bony hand of death is prying,
At their souls full of fear

The Southern Cross fell from the sky
The lord wasn't there to hear their cries
The black star blocking the sun
Men die by their own guns

Nevermore the sun will shine
As the souls walk down the line
The land of darkness, the sea of flame
All of them, never to breathe again

Johnny

My son,

My heart,

My soul.

At one time we were so close,

But now we are so far apart!

It is not your fault,

Nor is it mine.

It is the confusion that has been put into your mind.

Our love is deep,

So I know in time it will run that deep once again!

The Reality of Truth

I climbed the highest mountain on earth
Where breathing is hard 'because the air is thin
I watched as the sun gave daytime its birth
I watched people play games they can not win

Wars to the left of me, wars to the right
Poverty, hunger, ignorance and pain
My heart told me it was time to fight
As blood fell from the sky on me like rain

The mountain began to crumble and fall
A mighty wind carried me to the sea
People used the stones to build a wall
To protect themselves from reality

I swam ashore seeking comfort and aid
Only the truth came from behind the wall
As I got down on my knees and prayed
In the far distance I heard a faint call

Around the wall the truth and I did walk
In search of the voices heard crying out
People tried to confuse me with talk
Of things they really knew nothing about

People tried to suppress the truth from me
Again, my heart said it was time to fight
It was the children who began to see
The wall they built was more wrong than right

It was the voices of children that I heard
The wall made the truth hard for them to see

But the truth has whispered to them this word
No Wall Can Keep out Love's Reality

The Road

Time will let you understand,
Or it may not.
Sometime you take a chance on life!
Life never takes the turn you expect,
But it does take a road.
The road it takes is the most unexpected.
When you come to the end,
You never take the easy road,
You take the road with the most ups, downs and turns,
Because that road is what makes you who you are.

Have You Ever Walked a Long, Hard Mile?

Have you ever felt lonely
Lost, without a friend
You reach out your hand
But, there's no message to send

Have you ever cried
In the dark all alone
You look in the mirror
But your smile has flown

Have you ever seen blackness
Surrounding your life
You want a piece of the action
But you have no knife

Have you ever screamed
In the middle of the night
You think it's a dream
But it's right there in sight

Have you ever heard laughter
Felt secure with a smile
You can and will go on
But, that was a long, hard mile

A Short Road

Walking down this road
Looking for peace of mind
Love and friendship
I must find

You're on the same road
Together we'll see
The peace and joy
That friends can be

The Mind

Depression, suicide, mental illness, anxiety
These are problems in our society
The pay of our educators always does increase
Yet, none of these things seem to decrease

There are eating disorders and self-mutilation
I would help them all without hesitation
The mind is complex and very wonderful
It does need help in times that are sorrowful

The pentagon and trade centers struck by a plane
Who could imagine this act so insane
The mind is complex and very wonderful
It can make our love even more bountiful

The Hardest Thing to Do

Staring back at you
Eyes in the mirror
Do they belong to you
Are they getting clearer

Looking inside of you
Is so very hard
Deep down inside of you
Love you with deep regard

Touching the real you
Glorious and Grande
Accepting you as you
Is when you understand

Darkness

I had in my arms the gift of life, but before I could see the truth it
drifted away.

The sun came and the sun went as the days go by.

I thought I seen the light but once again all there was—was
darkness—Darkness that I could never overcome.

Taking The Time

I took a smile,
>   And turned it into a rainbow

I took laughter,
>   And turned it into world wide peace

I took a frown,
>   And planted its seed for it to grow

I took this growth,
>   So ugly, all frowns did cease

I took some love,
>   And offered it all around

I took some more,
>   And still had plenty to give

I took some time,
>   And the years went round and round

I'll take the time,
>   'Cause I still have plenty to give

The Pit (May)

For several days the rain has fallen
Everything is wet and soggy
Lookin' for a dry spot, worms are crawlin'
In my mind it is very foggy

A friend who was hurt, called on me
I spent last winter in a deep, dark pit
But, I had been there before, you see
I told my friend she must never quit

Depression is an enemy of mine
Out of its darkness, I have brought light
A smile and laughter from time to time
Only with love can I win the fight

Domestic violence is what they call it
It creates this enemy of mine
With some common sense and my wallet
If you're in the pit, I've got the time

Getting Out of the Pit

Life has come, life has gone
Some day, you will find what you are looking for
Until then, life is not what it seems
For life has so much more to offer

If you can only find your path through life
Some find it and some do not
Those who do not find only turmoil and death
The death of their existence

They can not find a way out
But for those who do
God Bless!
God Bless!

Death

You once said you loved me,
But now you say you want to kill me!
What should I believe?
One or the other they both mean the same.
In your eyes both are the same.
I will not go back no matter what you say,
Because both are death to me.
In your hands I would lay!

Life

Life is to live,
Life is to die!
Life is what you make it.
Life is what others give you,
Life is what others take from you,
But never what they give you!
They steal, they take,
But yet they expect so much in return,
But they never return only take,
Then they destroy!
Destroy the light they brought to this earth,
And then deny!

Poetic Love

My friend and room mate died from cancer
We shared his last two years
Love, I will always enhance her
To ease people's pain and fears

I have talked with victims of incest
To me they did reveal
But not to their psychiatrist
Truths that seem unreal

Wisdom comes to those who pray
Poetry has the power to heal
When your mind is frazzled and frayed
Poetic Love can be unreal!

Share With Me, Please

So many feelings inside of you
So many thoughts, you can not decide
So much confusion, making you blue
Allow me, please, to see you inside

Our feelings are shared by one and all
Our thoughts are our strength to help us strive
To end the confusion, once and for all
Show me, please, your need to be alive

So many feelings deep down inside
So many thoughts running round in your head
So much confusion, distorting your pride
Share with me, please, the thoughts in your head

My Little Girl, Desiree

I know a precious little girl
Sweet as sugar/cinnamon swirl
Her laughter and her pretty smile
Have carried me for many miles

In half a cabin made of log
On the mountain where we walked my dog
I listened to her while she talked
My tears came down as we walked

On Christmas Morn', she got a sled
Santa brought it right to her bed
We took that sled out in the snow
And her pretty face began to glow

These are memories of my good friend
Our time together had to end
She's grown a bit since way back then
I pray to God I'll see her again

My love for her I can not hide
All her feelings were trapped inside
Feelings and emotions fight to escape
From little girls who have been raped

Part II: The Visitation

As a young teen, she had a son
Like girls her age she thought it was fun
I pray I'll see her again some day
Too many women have lived this way

Part III: One Year Later

She's been in trouble with the law
A future for her that I saw
She does the best she can to live
Sins, of the innocent, God will forgive

Part IV: Life Goes On

She has been threatened with a knife
She will always cherish Life
I pray for her mother too
Her life was/is like this too

Part V: The Stolen Car

She's in prison, I read in the paper
Caught in a stolen car caper
God chose for me to be her friend
My love for her will never end

Part VI: The Letter

She's had two sons she can not see
She wrote in a letter to me
She's stopped writing, now I wait
To learn of her future fate

Part VII: She's in Heaven 6-18-2006

She died when she was twenty eight
God met her right at Heaven's Gate
I was like a father to her
She wrote me in the letter

Keep On Smilin'

Keep on smilin', the whole day through
Keep on smilin', what ever you do
Keep on smilin', when you're feeling down
Keep on smilin', share yourself around

When you are down, just find a friend
When you are down, it is not the end
When you are down, love is what you need
When someone's down, don't let them bleed

Keep on smilin', the world goes round
Keep on smilin', with friends you've found
Keep on smilin', be the real you
Keep on smilin', what ever you do

Growing

To seek and find what can be found
To know all that one mind can know
To listen and hear all the sounds
Follow dreams, where ever they go

These words go round and round inside
The mind that stops lies down to die
What is inside, please do not hide
The mind is vast, like a clear blue sky

To share and care with everyone
To sing and shout and laugh and play
Setting and rising of the sun
The mind grows vaster with each day

To Conquer

To dream is to see deep inside your heart
To cry is to show just the way you feel
To share is to give of your greatest part
The you inside that you know is for real

To search for your dream is hard to do
To feel the tears of others as they cry
The joy of sharing will always be with you
As long as your heart is willing to try

To find your dream is all you should hope for
And share with others tears of pain and joy
To share all that you have and even more
Loneliness and sorrow, you can destroy

Rainbow Lost

I look to myself for answers
Answers of why my love is not returned
For I held this love in my heart and soul since a child

When I spoke the truth of my love
I got no answers and no love was returned
I spoke of my love because I was led to believe
My love would some day be returned

In this turmoil of love not returned
What was I to do with my heart?
I try to go on, but it doesn't work
I see no light at the end of the rainbow

The rainbow does not exist for me
Not without this love that can not be seen
For it is a Lost Rainbow

The Angels or Me

My life, tried to be taken
    By my own hand
Three times I have tried
    I guess it was not meant to be
But, sometimes I think "should it be'
    Is my life worth saving?

To some it is not
    To some they say just die
Some say do not
    Whose advice should I take?
Who is right, who is wrong
    I hear both in the distance
Who is right?
    The angels or me

Inner Searches

The world came into view
And jumped back out again
Where was it going to
I had to ask a friend

My friend did not know where
We both chased after it
The world, it was not there
We searched and searched for it

Behind planets and stars
Other side of the sun
When we came home form Mars
A new search had now begun

The world is deep within
The inner depths of you
Happiness will begin
When you know the real you

Another Search

I searched the whole world over
For wisdom and truth I did seek
With each stone that I turned over
I became physically weak

Exhaustion crept in on me
So I had to stop my searching
There was so much yet to see
The truth for which I was searching

I had to stop and clear my mind
I found more than I bargained for
There was so much truth I had to find
I wondered what I did this for

Truth and wisdom, I have little
If I could live forever
I would still have just a little
Of all that there is together

Together, such a lovely wold
Together, all I had searched for
Together is the only word
That all of us should search for

Shell

I asked for help in my time of need
But there was no one there to help me
So I will never ask for help again
For no one can help me but me

I found that I need no one
Because no one can help me but me
There are no friends, there is no me
Only the shell that was once me

S.O.S.

Were you ever brought to confusion
Thought your mind was falling apart
Found life nothing but an illusion
And sorrow took control of your heart

Did you ever find that you were lost
And all roads lead to a dead end
The brightest lights were covered with frost
You could not see who was a friend

Do you know how to send up a flare
One that can be seen by a friend
Can you offer to God a prayer
Because He alone is your best friend

Fear I (6-4-1980)

Were you ever scared
Afraid of your own shadow
Unable to cope with life
Look for a friend
Hold their hand
And fear will leave
But if no one is there
Think of a friend
Imagine holding their hand
And fear will leave
For love is present

Fear II (5-14-1984)

Fear is so very strong
It does sneak up on you
Never right, nor is wrong
Fear does what it must do

Tremble and shake outside
Goose bumps are on your arms
Tremble and shake inside
Fear is using its charms

Feel your heart beat faster
Your eyes grow very wide
Nearing a disaster
Fear comes from the inside

External things are not
What brings about such fear
The inner things you've wrought
Created the fear that appears

Now, feel your spirit climb
It tramples down your fear
Do you think you have the time
To spread good will and cheer

Why

Why?
Why should I ask why
I brought what is on me on me
I have no one to blame
But yet, I still ask why

Why is the question
Who can answer me?
No one
But, I still ask why
Why will be the question until I die?

Time

Time is a state of mind
Time is a misconception of the mind!
A circle that goes around and round,
But it all comes back to the beginning and never ends.
That is the time in life.

Time

Circles going round and round
Mazes deep inside the mind
Where confusion often is found
And emotions begin to grind

New questions arise each day
Answers go on without end
Loneliness often does stay
Until the presence of a friend

What goes on inside the mind?
Is not to be hidden there
Love is like a clock you wind
That ticks along with friends who care

Guided Dream

Close your eyes
Drift away
Beautiful Places
Yes you may

Dream away
It feels so good
Getting away
From the neighborhood

You alone
Or with a friend
Dreams and reality
Together you'll blend

Come back home
Open your eyes
Feeling better
Bright blue skies

The thought by me
The dream for you
Love is present
In all you do

Finding Yourself

You've found some answers
And started to look
Finding the real you
Is like writing a book

You've got it together
Feeling so great
Some one stops by
And opens a gate

Before you can close it
Part of you slips away
Starting all over
Facing each day

Don't feel discouraged
You do have friends
Some who are searching
Some with time to lend

It will take time
A lesson to learn
Follow the light
It will always burn

Untitled

Sometimes it happens,
Sometimes it just stays the same.
Life comes,
Life goes.
Sometimes it's all about everything in between,
Or everything around us.
Sometimes one we love is lost,
Life gives,
And life takes,
But it's the life we live in between!
Life is a circle of events,
Ups, downs,
And all the in betweens that come and go!
All that is taken,
All that is given is what our lives are.
People judge,
People talk,
But no one has walked a day in your shoes.
So life is what you see in it!
Life is what you make it!
There is no in between only the truth,
In it or the lies people like to tell about it.

Confusion Inside

What is this feeling inside
That follows you night and day
All the times you have cried
Because it will not go away

When some one mentions the words
Your mind swiftly falls apart
It flies around like the birds
Taking with it your heart

Life is full of confusion
And it makes you wonder why
Love is not an illusion
It often makes you cry

Nothing

You see a child
You see an adult
Are they the same?
Or do they become two different people
What ever you see,
They are the same
The child within,
The child that they never let live
They stole what she had
Now all that is left is the empty soul they all threw away and left
  behind
Left behind to live alone and die alone!
Because to them she was just something to use
Just something that was never wanted
SO what does that make her?
NOTHING to them
But not to her?

Being Has Purpose

I went out for a stroll one day
Not watching where it was I was
I discovered I'd lost my way
I lost my way, just because

I wandered around aimlessly
Not knowing where it was I was
I took my stroll carelessly
I went on a stroll just because

I felt I had let myself down
Not liking where it was I was
I had brought to myself a frown
I brought myself down, just because

I soon found a way that I knew
Not losing where it was I was
I learned something I thought I knew
I am not alive, just because

Creatures and Cars

At the edge of the forest
Creatures and cars
Sounds of the night
Gazing at the stars

Reminiscing with a friend
Having a good time
Valleys of memories
Bright futures to climb

Animals and insects
Breathing in the night
Fears shall retreat
Hold on tight

A distant humming
The speeding cars
Life's a journey in time
Marked with battle scars

Gloom is Doomed

Each leaf has a magical shape
Blown gently in a summer breeze
Do you think you can relate
With the truth surrounding these

The sun rises every day
The moon and stars come out at night
Forget about the clouds so grey
Or the times when things were not right

Remember when you wore a smile
Think of those for whom you care
Live life in your own style
Thank you for the time you share

Share yourself with everyone
Don't keep your love inside of you
Turn those grey clouds into fun
See the wonders that love can do

Cards

My words no one hears
My soul no one sees
When will someone see?
Maybe being seen for what you really are is not in the cards of life
So all you can do is deal with the cards that were dealt to you,
Even if you don't want them,
They are all you have to hold on to,
Because you just don't have anything else
Nothing to hold,
Nothing to have,
Nothing to love,
Just what cards give you?
It's just the luck of the draw.

Keep Looking Straight Ahead

Look behind your head
And back in front again
Keep looking straight ahead
A motion that was them

Look back in life ten years
Think of ten years further
Count all of your fears
Confusion stretching further

Look outside your window
Looks back in the mirror
Listen to the wind blow
Making your mind clearer

Look back on all the smiles
Look forward to some more
Accept the hardest miles
There are more of them in store

Wrong or Right

Lost by my family in my
     Time of need
Imprisoned by wrong
     That fell on me
They did not see for a time
     When they saw, they could not save me
I know no wrong,
     I may know no right
Who could say what is wrong
     Or what is right

Post Abortion Syndrome ('79-1983)

Thanksgiving was a special day
We shared for several years
We talked and laughed and games did play
Never knowing of her fears

She felt at ease being with me
Something she had to remember
I'd learn the truth eventually
About this day in November

At sweet sixteen, she lost her child
The doctor took her child away
My phone number she always dialed
To ease her suffering that day

On the day before Thanksgiving
The abortion did occur
She knew her life was worth living
My friendship, God gave to her

How free is Freedom?

She was murdered while posing for pictures
Canadian porn actress Natel King
She chose the stage name Taylor Sumers
How many have died while doing their "thing"

The Supreme Court has said it was freedom
Miss King came to the states 'because it is "free"
How many others have died like she did
They sought to be free and they no longer "be"

Porn Addiction Vs. We the People

They sit and watch the whole day through
And they dream and dream and dream
Their problems just grew and grew and grew
And every day the children scream

Betrayed and conquered by those they know
Their problems just grew and grew and grew
But the Supreme Court told them all no
Porn pushers can do what it is they do

They will not protect "We the People"
The children's pain is felt by my soul
Some may say the court is evil
Or maybe they practice mind control

Pregnancy Test Kit

In restroom stalls at a fast food place
In privacy, so no one will see
They learn of the future they face
Is there now a child that will be

They have no one they can trust who cares
They are scared, lonely and confused
They feel everyone stops and stares
When needed most, friendship is refused

It's so easy to create life
It seems so good it can't be wrong
To be a parent, husband and wife
Both mind and soul must be very strong

Detour

I fell into a hole today
No one was there to help me
I knelt down on my knees to pray
Hoping some one would set me free

The minutes turned into hours
While I knelt in the slime and muck
The skies were filled with rain showers
And I started to believe in luck

Bad luck was all I found this day
Covered with mud, stuck in a hole
But I knew bad luck would not stay
Nothing can keep me from my goal

I know there is no luck at all
Neither bad, good, or in between
So, if into a hole you fall
Think of the good times to be seen

II

Hope

"Pleasant words are like a honeycomb, sweetness to the soul and health to the body."

Proverbs 16:24

Hope in the Darkness

In the deepest, darkest part of the mind
Is found confusion, depression and fear
Ignorance controls feelings of this kind
The truth is something no one wants to hear

Cross through the darkness to the other side
Many light years beyond the end of time
Be purified of all your earthly pride
And comprehend the reason for this rhyme

Self-centeredness creates darkness and hate
Something in life all of us must face
A reality that is more than fate
It is part of "Being" the human race

Touched

I have touched on life
That will never touch on me
Friends that have taken me for granted
That will not touch me

They could not see the real me
But when they see the real me
They will not believe the friend
They could have had in me
When will they see?

When it is too late to conceive
For when I am gone
And they know what they have done wrong
They will wish they could have known
The real me, the friend in me

Minds That Do

A gathering of thoughts brought forth a pen
And I did something never done before
I keep doing it again and again
Gatherings of thoughts for all to explore

Gatherings of thoughts with rhythm and rhyme
Soul to mind to paper to pen to you
Thoughts to make minds think throughout all time
Turning minds that think into minds that do

Gather some thoughts and see what you can do
Too many wise minds forget how to share
These words have been written for me and you
Minds that are doing are minds that care

Heart

I fell to my knees,
    Because I need what you can give me
But because of my mistakes,
    In my hard times, you cannot see me

These are my times
    That only I can see
If only you could see
    You would be able to forgive
The bad and wrong in me

If only you could see
    The heart in me

Does, Did

Did you ever stop and wonder
About your feelings deep inside
Does the lighting and thunder
Make you search for a place to hide

Did you ever lie in bed at night
And try to stop your flowing tears
Does the world at times bring you fight
And make you think of you past years

Did you ever think about time
And how your life goes on and on
Does your thinking follow this rhyme
Or do you think it is a con

Did you ever look at a friend
And see inside the same as you
Does your life, this message send
You and I, together, can do

Truth of Me

When I am without you
    I am truly alone
When I am with you
    I am never alone
Even for an hour at a time
    The time with you is never
Spent alone

Alone I will always be
    Because you never give me the time I need
Because of the things that people say
    Because of the things you hear
But you never ask me to say,
    So you will never see the truth of me

You Don't Have to Impress Anyone

I reached out with my hand
And grabbed a bunch of stars
And with my other hand
Took a hold of Mars

I juggled them awhile
It was a sight to see
No one around me smiled
They walked away from me

A feat no one had done
They did not care to see
I thought it would be fun
For all on earth to see

I put the stars in place
Put Mars where it should be
Each and every face
Smiles, 'cause I am me

Do It!

It's your life
It all depends on you
Your dreams can come true
If only you believe

Don't sit around
Get up off you butt
Start things moving
Stop waiting

You're the one—Come, get started
Make your own life—Do it!

The Rhythm of Rhymes

Hello, my friend, how are you
Did you understand your thoughts today
Crazy thoughts, I have them too
Let's talk awhile, hear what we say

Thoughts go on inside the mind
Thoughts that seem distant and far
Thoughts with meanings hard to find
Thoughts that twinkle like a star

We all have thoughts, don't you know
We all get confused at times
We all get to feeling low
We all need the rhythm of rhymes

Relax

We all need some time to relax
Be with friends and forget our cares
Take all the weight off our backs
A good time that everyone shares

Life is a journey everyday
Labor and toil to earn our keep
The time friends share at work and play
The roots of love are very deep

Memories are a special part
Of all that we are and shall be
They often help strengthen our heart
And understand reality

Precious Moments

Twisting round in the wind
Floating with ocean waves
Tumbling down with the rain
Precious moments to save

A smile here and a smile there
A friendly joyous hello
Dancing here and singing there
Moments never to let go

Friendly conversation
Understanding inside
A place where one can rest
Moments never to hide

Sharing, caring and more
A total sacrifice
Nothing asked in return
Moments that makes up life

Miracles

Each minute, of every hour, of each day
Miraculous, glorious, things abound
We walk, talk, and hear what others say
Never thinking of the love to be found

A smile, laughter, or a simple "Hello"
Miracles like these we fail to see
The glory of God, above and below
A miracle is not a mystery

The greatest miracle of all is life
The plants, animals, and people too
We can overcome our moments of strife
If living and loving is all we do

The mirror reflects the miracle of you
Take this miracle, and show it around
Live, love and work at whatever you do
Share the miracle of you that you've found

The Well Digger

Woke up just today
With warmth I hope will stay
Feeling like I ought to kiss the world and cry

Right in the palm of my hand
There's a message for every land
Send me your ears and I'll tell you why

There's a role I can fill
Pain and sorrow I can kill
Please, won't you give me a try

Just reach out your hand
I'll try to understand
Then I'll take you to the sky

With one look I can tell
I'll go deep down in your well
And I can see love in you eyes

Hands of Peace

A hand reached out and held onto mine
My other hand reached out for another
Spiritual food with which to dine
When we prove our love for another

We will hold a circle, the whole world round
Our hands will hold onto another's
Love, peace, and joy can be found
When we give of ourselves for another

Suns Delight

When life gets you down, don't break down. Look to the better side
of life.

There is always one there if you look hard, and look inside yourself.

When the day is filled with rain & gloom, and the fog rolls in with the
night

Remember the next day will be filled with the suns delight

III

Love

"…, so surely my friend shall forever be my friend, and reflect a ray of God to me, and time shall foster and adorn and consecrate our friendship, no less than the ruins of temples.
As I love nature, as I love singing birds, and gleaming stubble, and flowing rivers, and morning and evening, and summer and winter, I love thee my friend."

From: "A Week on the Concord and Merrimack Rivers." By: Henry David Thoreau

Stars of Love

I see the stars
But the stars do not see me
For I am lost
Lost I will always be

Until I find my love
I will be incomplete
Until my love finds in himself
To find me

Sensational

Create a little magic using words
Draw me a nest of singing birds
Bring all the clouds down out of the sky
Is love really the twinkle in you eye

Show me the smile of a happy child
The swiftness of a rabbit running world
Envision the colors of the rainbow
Does love come out of your halo

Let me hear the sound of children at play
Help me enjoy all the words you say
Describe for me your feelings inside
Is love the strength that is your guide

Let me touch and feel the beauty of you
Describe the sensation of thoughts anew
Let's try to know the spirit of the heart
Know that love is your most important part

Fallen Love

Your beautiful smile is like a ray of sunshine beaming down on me
    warming my soul. Without your love in my life it is no life at all.
So this day our love brings me happiness with every rise & fall without
    you I could have never loved at all.

To JDM who I will always love!

When You Left

You left one night in the pouring rain. You were never seen again. To my surprise our love was gone and never to be seen again.

It came upon a day we crossed each others path. Neither could speak because we could not forget the past.

My tears I held back because I could not let you see, because my life is empty when there is no you & me.

Legs

My friend who left me too soon.

My friend who should have never been taken.

How do I forgive my guilt that has been drowning my heart and soul?

I can no longer live with my guilt,

But only be forgiven for what I feel is my wrong.

Please god forgive me,

Because I can not forgive myself.

I could have stopped this death,

But am I wrong?

No one knows,

But the one I did wrong. I ask for forgiveness for the one I did wrong.

To S.K. who will always be missed.

Day by Day

The sun goes up and the sun goes down
And in between the whole world goes round
The stars come out and the moon does shine
And God's love makes the world so fine

Life is so long, and short, all the same
Tempting us all with riches and fame
Love is the heart of each girl and boy
Tempting us all with sorrow and joy

Time is a friend that guides us with age
Life is a book and each day a page
The gift of love is seen in a smile
Life is a road with many a mile

The sun goes up and the sun goes down
At times a smile will turn to a frown
The stars come out and the moon does shine
The love in us all makes life so fine

Friends

Friends are sorrows
Friends are joys
Some are girls
And some are boys

Friends are laughter
Friends are fun
Be a friend
And listen to "Gun" (my nickname)

Friends are love
Friends are forever
We all can be friends
And live life together

Friend & Family

My friend, my family
The only one who would help me?
No matter what he says you still help me.
Thank you for that, no matter what disbeliefs we have,
You still and always will stand behind me. Thank You

She Said She Had Crawled Out From the Grave

She had been abused for many years
Defiantly, she brought it to an end
After all of the pain and all the tears
She had to go out and find a friend

She said she had crawled out from the grave
She had now begun a new way of living
All alone when she crawled out from the grave
Family and friends denied their giving

God sent her to the home of a special friend
I helped to ease her pain and fear
Her damaged soul then began to mend
She knows that God will always be near

The Old and the New

When you first came to me, your mind was a real mess
And I had some mental problems of my own.
The pain of your nightmares helped heal my loneliness
Some of the longest nights I have ever known

The mess in your mind has slowly begun to clear
My mind is filled with knowledge I've gained from you
When I think of your pain, my eyes begin to tear
Enjoy all the good times in your life a new!

Giggles

When you're feelin' good,
    The giggles arrive
And a great big smile
    Comes to your face
When you're feelin' good,
    Happy thoughts arrive
And a great big smile
    Comes to your face

When you're feelin' good,
    Your spirit shines
And a great big smile
    Comes to your face
When you're feelin' good,
    My spirit shines
And a great big smile
    Comes to my face

To my Reader

Ten minutes have gone by
I still do not know why
No words can come to me
To make a poem to be

These words are all around
Their meaning to be found
Together they can make
A world without mistake

When these words settle in
Joy and peace will begin
Their message plain and true
I really do love you

In Closing

So you want to know the score
Well listen very hard
Material things are bore
That's my greeting card

Money keeps me going
That's all I need it for
See, your smile is showing
Love, is truly life's core

Fun is all that matters
Sharing a smile or two
Success ain't found on ladders
It's in making friends like you!

About the Author: Mike Rother

As a youth, the public library was my home away from home. I attended Catholic school for twelve years, and then I studied accounting for 3 1/2 semesters. A personal experience I had during the winter of 1977-'78, made me realize things would be the way they are today. I foresaw a nation plagued with a multitude of "social-psychological" problems. I "dropped out" before I "flunked out" and went out into the street to get an "education." These words are for the victims of abuse. Poetry has the power to Heal!

Thanks to Kathy's son Johnny Trevorah for his poem "End of The World"

About the Co-Author: Kathy

No one knows what life will bring. The best you can do is make the best of the bad and hope for better things to come. I have had a lot of bad and have seen a lot of bad, but I always hope for better, not only for me, but for the rest of the world.

978-0-595-47577-3
0-595-47577-9

www.ingramcontent.com/pod-product-compliance
Lightning Source LLC
Chambersburg PA
CBHW051257050326
40689CB00007B/1227